KI

VF

COOK BOOK

KINGS PANTRY

VEGETARIAN COOK BOOK

VALERIE CHAZAN

Illustrations by Helen Herbert

SILENT BOOKS
Cambridge

Acknowledgements

Without the encouragement of my three, now grown-up, children, The Kings Pantry would not exist. So it is to Yigal, Sharon and Guy that I say thank you. I would also like to give heartfelt thanks to my staff, especially Irene my manageress, without whom this would not have been possible.

There is provision made in this book for you to record your own recipes or variations.

First published in Great Britain 1986
by Silent Books, Swavesey, Cambridge CB4 5RA

© 1986 Valerie Chazan

ISBN 1 85183 002 2

Typeset by Goodfellow & Egan
Printed in Great Britain by
Richard Clay (The Chaucer Press) Ltd,
Bungay, Suffolk

Contents

Recipes

Starters

Sharon's avocado dip	19
Avocado starter	19
Asparagus on toast	20
Stuffed eggs	20
Humus and tahini	21
Tuna and apple	21

Salads

Beetroot salad	22
Cucumber salad	23
Flageolet beans with cottage cheese	24
Rice salad	25
Mushroom salad	25
Fresh potato salad	26
Red cabbage salad	27
Carrot and orange salad	27
Piqmant carrot salad	28
Tomato salad	28
Traditional coleslaw	28
Celeriac salad	29
Bulgar wheat salad	29

Vegetable side dishes

Sweet and sour cabbage	30
Potato latkes or fritters	30
Baked sweet potato or yams	31
Tyneside fried leeks	32
Fennel in white sauce	32
Broccoli in cheese sauce	33
String beans in tomato sauce	33
Jane's hot dutch brown beans	34
Egyptian foule beans	35

Main courses

Soya bean loaf	36
Lentil croquettes	37
Leek and cheddar flan	37
Aubergine flan or bake	38
Sweetcorn flan	38
Boracas	39
Bean and cheese loaf	40
Stuffed cabbage encroûte	41
Potato and apple bake	42

Desserts

Cakes and biscuits

Health drinks

The Kings Pantry

The Kings Pantry is situated in the city of Cambridge, England. It stands right opposite Kings College in her most famous street – Kings Parade. Preparing food for large numbers of people has always been easy and enjoyable for me. Thus, when the derelict basement of a listed building was made available to me, opening a restaurant seemed a natural progression from cooking for the family and The Kings Pantry was born. We have been established now for 4 years, and have acquired a reputation for good wholesome food of which we are very proud. In the Pantry I have used and adapted my recipe collection gathered over many years to create a wholefood and vegetarian restaurant enjoyed by locals, students and tourists alike. We were chosen by the Vegetarian Society to be in their 'Pick of the Year' for 1985, and are moving over to be totally vegetarian in 1986.

The recipes in this book have been collected over 30 years. They have been used and adapted by me to suit my needs; a large number have been created out of the need to provide variety for my vegetarian family. Some have been borrowed from friends and staff, and acknowledged in the title of each. The oldest recipe dates from the Second World War, a marvellous economical recipe for almond flan that utilises old or stale cake. They have an international flavour, but all the ingredients are available in Britain. The recipes provide a base from which to start, and it is hoped that you will experiment with the ingredients, to create nourishing food that suits your own taste and requirements.

Valerie Chazan

Basic Recipes

Pastry making

Shortcrust

Ingredients for 1 lb
1 lb (450 g)   Flour (half
wholemeal, half self-raising)
½ lb (225 g)   Margerine
½ teaspoon   Salt
3–6 tablespoons   Water

Throughout the book the following basic short-crust pastry is used unless otherwise stated. It can be made by hand or machine. In the machine more water needs to be added to make the pastry dough soft enough to roll out. In the restaurant we use a mixture of wholemeal and white self-raising flour. This makes the pastry light. Adding more flour also makes the pastry lighter.

Method

Sift the flour and salt. Rub the fat into the flour. Add enough cold water to make a pastry dough. Chill for 1 hour before rolling out.

When making flans or pies in tins with straight sides it is a good idea to roll a thin snake and tuck it into the bed of the tin to prevent leaking. Prick the base.

When making pies, prick the lid and paint it with beaten egg, milk or cream. In a savoury pie a little cheese can be sprinkled on the top or on a sweet pie, sugar (preferably demerera).

9

Puff pastry

This pastry is used for such delicacies as vol-au-vents, boracus and strudels. Making it is a time consuming process so therefore I recommend buying the frozen variety and keeping it handy in the freezer. It is generally very good quality and no-one would know you hadn't made it yourself. Make sure you take it out of the freezer a few hours before use. Roll it out quite thinly.

Salad Dressings

Basic vinegar dressing

Ingredients
⅔ pint (400 ml)   White or wine vinegar
4 oz (125 g)   White sugar
Salt and pepper to taste

Method

Mix well. The best way to do this is to put the mixture into a coffee jar with a screw lid, and shake well until the sugar is dissolved.

Kings Pantry french dressing

Ingredients
⅔ pint (400 ml)   White or wine vinegar
4 oz (125 g)   White sugar
1 dessertspoon   French Mustard
Salt and pepper to taste

Method

Prepare in the same way as basic vinegar dressing.

Mayonnaise

This recipe is made in the blender bowl of the food processor. It is extremely simple.

Ingredients
1   Egg
1 pint (600 ml)   Oil
1 tablespoon   Vinegar
1 teaspoon   Mustard (optional)
Salt and pepper to taste

Method

Put half the vinegar and the eggs in the blender, While the blender is working pour the oil very slowly onto the blades until the mixture becomes thick and creamy. Add the remaining vinegar and the salt and pepper. A little lemon juice or mustard can be added. Store in a jar in the fridge where it will keep very well.

Sauce preparation: the roux

Ingredients for basic sauce
2 oz (50 g)   Margarine or butter
2 oz (50 g)   Plain white flour
1 pint (600 ml)   Milk, water, wine or stock

A roux is a combination of fat, flour and liquid. The most important point in preparing the roux is the prevention of lumps by constant gentle stirring over a low heat.

The roux can be used as a basis for a whole variety of sauces which often have complicated French names. I just label them with the extra ingredients I add – such as cheese, capers, parsley, wine, cream, mushroom, mustard, horseradish, caraway or lemon. The sauce can be made as thick or thin as you wish by varying the amount of liquid added. The basic liquid can be milk, water, wine or stock. The strength of the sauce can also be varied by adding more or less of the extra ingredient.

The roux then is one of the most fundamental elements of cooking. It can dress meat, fish, vegetables, pasta and sweet dishes, or it can be used to refresh yesterday's leftovers.

Method

Melt the margarine or butter over a low heat, take care not to burn the bottom of the pan. Stir in enough plain flour to form a soft ball and absorb all the fat. Take the pan off the heat and slowly add half the milk, beat until smooth and then return to a low heat stirring all the time. Add the rest of the milk, raise the heat slightly until the sauce thickens and begins to boil, then reduce the heat and allow to simmer and cook for about 2 minutes. This is the basic sauce. Now you can thin it to taste, and add the different seasonings.

Soups

Pea and lentil soup

Ingredients for 6–8
4 oz (125 g)   Yellow split peas
4 oz (125 g)   Green lentils
3 pints (1800 ml)   Water
Salt and pepper to taste
1 teaspoon   Turmeric
1 dessertspoon   Soy sauce

This is a really hearty soup. Its ingredients can be altered to suit your taste, or whatever happens to be in the pantry. You can also vary the colour of the lentils. I add a handful of tinned canelloni and a handful of tinned borlotti beans which have been chopped a few seconds in the blender to the finished soup to add interest and strengthen the flavour. Sometimes I also add a teaspoon of curry powder. Serve with hot buttered, or garlic bread.

Method

Soak the peas and lentils overnight (except red lentils). Drain off the water and put them in a large saucepan. Add water to cover. Bring them to the boil and simmer until tender (about 2 hours). Blend for 2 minutes. Add all the other ingredients and simmer for a further 10 minutes. Season again to taste. Make up to 3 pints with water.

This soup thickens after 24 hours so add more water and reseason. It will keep for a week in the fridge and freezes well.

✓ Cream of mushroom soup

Ingredients for 4–6
4 oz (125 g) Margarine or butter
2 oz (50 g) Plain flour
2 pints (1200 ml) Milk
1 lb (450 g) Mushrooms, wiped
and broken into bite-size pieces.
2 teaspoons Dried mixed herbs
Salt and pepper to taste
Cream to serve

This soup, another invention of mine using a roux as the base, is really delicious. Some people prefer to blend the mushrooms. I prefer to leave them cut in pieces. A swirl of thin cream and a little chopped parsley makes an attractive garnish.

Method

Make a roux with the margarine, flour and milk (p.11). Add the broken mushrooms, salt, pepper and herbs and simmer for 5 minutes. If the soup is too thick add a little milk or water. Serve garnished with a swirl of cream and a little chopped parsley. Alternatively, tinned celery hearts can be blended with the roux instead of mushrooms. Add ¼ teaspoon cayenne pepper to taste.

This soup will keep in the fridge for 2 days and will freeze well.

✓ Cream of tomato soup

Ingredients for 6–8
2 oz (50 g) Margarine or butter
2 oz (50 g) Plain flour
2 pints (1200 ml) Milk
1 tablespoon Sugar
2 teaspoons Dried mixed herbs
14 oz (400 g) Can of plum
tomatoes
1–2 Crushed cloves of garlic
Salt and pepper to taste
Cream to serve

This soup can be dressed up with a swirl of cream and sprinkle of chopped fresh parsley. It was my first invention at The Kings Pantry and is still one of the favourite soups with a rich tomato taste.

Method

Make a roux with the margarine, flour and milk (p.11). Make a purée of the tomatoes in a blender. Add the puréed tomatoes, sugar, seasoning, herbs and garlic to the roux. Bring to the boil and simmer for 5 minutes. If the soup is too thick, add a little more milk or water. Serve with a swirl of cream and chopped parsley.

This soup will keep 2 days in the fridge and freezes well.

Leek and potato soup

Ingredients for 6–8
2 oz (50 g)   Margarine
8 oz (225 g)   Onions
1 lb (450 g)   Potatoes
2 lb (1 Kilo)   Leeks
3 pints (1800 ml)   Water
Salt and pepper to taste
1 dessertspoon   Dried basil

The leek season is quite long so this soup can be served throughout a good part of the year.

Method

Wash the leeks and cut into 1-inch pieces, peel and cube the onions and potatoes. Melt the margarine and fry the onions and leeks for 5 minutes stirring all the time. Cover with cold water. Bring to the boil, lower the heat and cook until soft (about 10 minutes). Blend for 2 minutes. Add the salt, pepper, basil and soy sauce. Make up to 3 pints with cold water. Bring to the boil, simmer for 5 minutes and serve with hot buttered bread. Alternatively, cooked celery hearts can replace the leeks.

It will keep well in the fridge for 2–3 days and freezes well.

Celery and vegetable soup

Ingredients for 6–8
1   Large onion
3 lb (1½ Kilos)   Mixed vegetables
(leeks, celery, carrots, peppers,
etc.)
4 oz (125 g)   Margarine
3 pints (1800 ml)   Water
1 dessertspoon   Soy sauce
A shake of chilli sauce
Salt and pepper
Fresh parsley to garnish

This soup is a real "What do we have in the cupboard?" soup. You need 3 lbs of mixed vegetables. If you add one large potato it will thicken it beautifully.

Method

Peel and dice the vegetables. Melt the margarine over a low heat. Gently fry the vegetables in the margarine for 5 minutes. Cover with water and bring to the boil. Simmer for 10 minutes. Blend for 1 minute so the vegetables are roughly chopped. Season to taste with the soy sauce, chilli sauce, salt and pepper. Make up to 3 pints with water. Bring to the boil. Serve with a sprinkle of chopped parsley.

Keeps several days in the fridge and freezes well.

Carrot soup

Ingredients for 6–8
2 lb (1 Kilo)   Carrots
1 lb (450 g)   Potatoes
8 oz (225 g)   Onions
2 pints (900 ml)   Milk
1 oz (50 g)   Sugar
2 oz (50 g)   Butter
Salt and pepper
1 teaspoon   Soy sauce
Cream and chopped parsley to
garnish

This is an excellent starter for a dinner party. It tastes wonderful and looks attractive – especially when garnished with cream and chopped parsley.

Method

Peel, slice and fry the onions in the butter until transparent. Add the peeled and cubed carrots and potatoes. Cover with 1 pint of milk and a little water. Bring to the boil and simmer for 10 minutes. Blend until smooth. Add the sugar, soy sauce, salt and pepper to taste. Bring back to the boil. Add the remaining milk and enough water to make up to 3 pints. Serve with a swirl of cream and chopped fresh parsley.

Keeps 2 days in the fridge and will freeze well.

Ros's watercress soup

Ingredients for 6–8
2 lb (1 kilo)   Potatoes, peeled and cubed
4 bunches   Watercress
3 pints (1800 ml)   Water
1 dessertspoon   Soy sauce

This is one of Ros's recipes (one of my staff – a great cook). It can be served hot or cold and looks attractive served with a swirl of cream.

Method

Before untying the bunches of watercress cut the roots off with scissors. Then swish the bunches around in a sink full of water to remove any grit. Put it into a pan with the potatoes containing 2 pints of boiling water. Simmer for 10 minutes then blend until smooth. Make up to around 3 pints with water depending on the thickness you require. Bring to the boil, add the soy sauce and season. Don't add milk to this as it will curdle, but serve with a swirl of cream.

This will keep in the fridge for 2–3 days. It will thicken so add more water and reseason. It can be frozen.

Beetroot bortsch

Ingredients for 4–6
2 lb (1 kilo)   Red beetroots
1   Large onion
1   Egg yolk
2 pints (900 ml)   Water
Juice of ½ lemon
1 dessertspoon   Sugar
1 dessertspoon   Soy sauce
Sour cream to garnish

This soup usually has a base of beef stock but it is not necessary. Bortsch can be served hot or cold. Either way, it is delicious with a large helping of sour cream.

Method

Peel and cut the beetroot into 2-inch cubes. Peel and slice the onion. Bring the beetroot and onion to the boil in 2 pints water, simmer for an hour or more until the beetroots are tender. Put the liquid through a sieve reserving a quarter of the beetroot. Grate this in the food processor. (The remaining beetroot can be used for a salad.) Return the grated beetroot to the soup together with the lemon juice, sugar and soy sauce. Season with salt and pepper. Bring to the boil and simmer for 5 minutes. Cool slightly and stir in the beaten egg yolk. Make sure the soup is not too hot or it will curdle. Serve with sour cream.

This will keep a few days in the fridge if served cold. It will freeze but only add the egg yolk when defrosted.

Cauliflower soup

Ingredients for 6–8
1   Large cauliflower
2 pints (900 ml)   Milk
1 dessertspoon   Soy sauce
1 teaspoon   Nutmeg
Salt and pepper
2 oz (50 g)   Grated cheddar cheese

Make this when cauliflowers are cheap. It is really filling and is a meal in itself when served with bread and butter. This goes down very well in the restaurant.

Method

Wash the cauliflower and break it into florets. If it isn't woody the stalk can be included. Discard the outer leaves. Bring to the boil with the milk, simmer for 10 minutes. Blend for a minute or two until smooth. Make up to around 3 pints with water. Add the soy sauce, mustard, salt and pepper. Fill a cup with the soup and mix in the grated cheese, return this to the soup. Serve hot with a sprinkle of nutmeg on the top.

It will keep 2 days in the fridge and will also freeze.

Fruit soup

Ingredients for 6–8
2 lb (1 kilo)   Fresh fruit (grapes,
melon, apples, plums, etc.)
2 oz (50 g)   Sultanas
Juice of 1 lemon
Sugar to taste
2 pints (1200 ml)   Water

This soup originates from Israel. I've not tasted it in Britain. It is delicious served with a swirl of fresh or sour cream, and it can be served thick or thin. When thinned down it becomes a lovely summer drink especially when served with ice. It is usually made from fresh fruit but it can be made from dried fruit (soaked 2–3 hours first) or tinned fruit (without the extra sugar). Of course you can use a combination. A glass of orange juice or wine can be added at the end and the flavour can be varied by adding cinnamon and cloves to the cooking. It can be thickened with a little cornflour

Method

Cut the fruit into small pieces. Boil in the water then skim the surface. Simmer for 10 minutes, dilute and add more sugar if necessary. Chill.

Keeps well in the fridge and freezes well.

Starters

Sharon's avocado dip

Ingredients for 2–4
1   Large avocado
2 tablespoons   Cottage cheese
1   Hard-boiled egg, chopped
2 cloves   Crushed garlic
2 dessertspoons   Plain yoghurt or mayonnaise
Good squeeze of lemon
1   Chopped tomato (optional)
Salt and pepper
Sprinkle of Cumin (optional)

Method

Remove the skin and stone from the avocado. Put all the ingredients in the blender for 2 minutes. Season and serve on a lettuce leaf garnished with tomato. Serve with crackers.

Make as needed.

Avocado starter

Ingredients for 4
2   Ripe avocado pears
Lemon juice
4 oz (50 g)   Strawberries (fresh or frozen)
Dash of sugar
Salt and pepper
Sour cream
Mint leaves to garnish

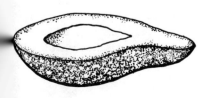

This is a simple dish which looks very colourful at a dinner party.

Method

Cut the avocado pears lengthwise and remove stone cover the surface with lemon juice to stop discolouration. Season lightly. Roughly chop the strawberries. Add a dash of sugar and lemon juice and fill the avocado halves with the mixture. Top with a whole strawberry and sour cream. Decorate with mint leaves.

Make as needed.

Asparagus on toast

Ingredients for 4
14 oz (400 g)   Asparagus tips
(tinned or fresh)
4 pieces of buttered toast with
crusts removed
2 oz (50 g)   Cheddar cheese
sliced into thin strips
Parsley to garnish

This is a very tasty starter which looks mouth-watering. You can use either tinned or fresh asparagus.

Method

If using fresh asparagus, simmer for 10 minutes in water. Remove the stems. Lay the asparagus tips side by side on the toast. Season lightly. Put the strips of cheddar across the asparagus. Grill for 5 minutes. Serve immediately, garnished with parsley.

Make as needed.

Stuffed eggs

Ingredients for 2
2   Hard-boiled eggs
1 teaspoon   Mayonnaise
1 teaspoon   Tomato ketchup
Dash of mustard
Dash of cumin
Salt and pepper
4 slivers of anchovy (to garnish)
Parsley and lettuce for decoration

This is a very simple dish that can be used as the basis of a salad plate.

Method

Slice the hard eggs lengthwise, scoop out the yolk and mix it together with the other ingredients. Fill the eggs and decorate with anchovies if wished. Serve on a lettuce leaf with a sprig of parsley on top.

Make as needed.

Humus and tahini

Ingredients for 6
7 oz (200 g)   Tin of prepared
humus (or make your own fresh)
7 oz (200 g)   Concentrated tahini
3 cloves   Crushed garlic
Paprika powder (Pinch)
Juice from lemon
Salt and pepper
A variety of sour pickle to garnish

This is a very filling high-protein dish which can be served as a starter or as a meal in itself accompanied by hot pitta bread and sour pickles. It is a Middle Eastern staple.

Method

When mixed with water tahini paste forms an emulsion. Put the tahini in a bowl and add water a little at a time mixing briskly until the tahini forms a smooth cream. It will double its quantity. To this add lemon juice, crushed garlic, salt and pepper to taste. Spread 2 tablespoons of this cream over the surface of a tea plate. Put a good dessertspoon of humus from the tin on the centre. Decorate with pieces of pickled cucumber, olives, onions or pickled peppers and pinch paprika powder.

This keeps for 2 days only in the fridge.

Tuna and apple

Ingredients for 4–6
14 oz (400 g)   Tin of tuna in oil
or brine
2   Red eating apples
4 oz (125 g)   Mayonnaise
Salt and pepper

This colourful dish is very quick to prepare. It is not only useful as a starter but it is also excellent in vol-au-vent cases or sandwiches.

Method

Drain the oil or brine from the tuna and chop it up finely. Core the apple and leave the skin on and cut into tiny cubes. Mix all the ingredients together with the mayonnaise. You may find that salt and pepper are not necessary.

It will stay fresh in the fridge for 2–3 days.

Salads

Beetroot salad

Ingredients for 6–8
2 lb (1 kilo)   Raw or tinned beetroot
Basic vinegar dressing (p.10)
1   Chopped onion (optional)
Salt and pepper

This is an excellent standby recipe. Tinned whole beetroots in salt water are used since they are of very good quality. If you wish to use fresh beetroots then boil them with their skins on until tender. Cover them in cold water and peel the skin. We were brought up on this salad. It is lovely in a cheese sandwich and a good accompaniment to cold meat dishes.

Method

Chop the beetroot roughly. Season with salt and pepper. Add the onion and enough prepared vinegar dressing to cover. Marinade for 24 hours in the fridge before serving. As an alternative, cover the cut beetroot with a 5 fl. oz (150 ml) carton of plain yoghurt and add 1 teaspoon of cumin (this will only keep for 3 days in the fridge).

Here I offer you 3 easy cucumber salads. They are tasty, quick to prepare and ideal to serve at a buffet.

Laura's cucumber salad

Ingredients for 4
1   Large cucumber
4 oz (125 g)   Sugar
8 fl oz (225 ml)   White wine vinegar
Salt and pepper

Method

Deeply scratch the cucumber from top to bottom, with a fork – this gives an attractive serrated look to the finished dish. Now top and tail the cucumber finely slice by hand or in the food processor. Dissolve the sugar in the vinegar and marinade the cucumber for 1 hour before serving.

Will keep 2 days in the fridge.

Cucumber salad

Ingredients for 4
1   Large cucumber
1   Small banana
5 fl oz (150 ml)   Plain yoghurt
2 cloves   Crushed garlic
Salt and pepper

Method

Thinly slice the banana and cucumber, add the yoghurt, garlic, salt and pepper to taste and a teaspoon of sugar if wished. Marinade for 1 hour before serving.

This will keep 2 days in the fridge.

Cucumber salad

Ingredients for 4
1   Cucumber
1 tablespoon   Honey
2 tablespoons   Water
2 tablespoons   White wine vinegar
1 teaspoon   Chopped dill
Salt and pepper

Method

Thinly slice the cucumber. Mix the remaining ingredients and add to the cucumber. Marinade for 1 hour before serving.

This will keep for 2 days in the fridge.

Ros's bean salad

Ingredients for 8–10
14 oz (400 g)   Tin red kidney
beans (rinsed)
14 oz (400 g)   Tin white kidney
beans (rinsed)
14 oz (400 g)   Tin cut french
beans (drained)
1   Small green pepper (diced)
1   Small red pepper (diced)
1   Small onion (diced)
6 oz (175 g)   White sugar
6 fl oz (175 ml)   White wine
vinegar
2 fl oz (50 ml)   Corn oil
½ teaspoon   French mustard
Salt and pepper

This salad was enjoyed by everyone attending one of Ros's parties so I pinched the recipe. It is very colourful and keeps well. It is good served at a hot or cold meal and is very filling.

Method

Mix all the ingredients together and marinade for 24 hours.

The flavour improves with keeping in the fridge. It will keep for about a week.

Flageolet beans with cottage cheese

Ingredients for 4–6
14 oz (400 g)   Tin flageolet beans
2 cloves   Crushed garlic
½ teaspoon   Dried cumin
1   Chopped hard-boiled egg
4 oz (125 g)   Cottage cheese
Juice of ½ lemon
Salt and pepper

Flageolet beans are tender and sweet and have a lovely green colour. The recipe uses tinned beans, but if using dried you must prepare in advance by soaking them for 48 hours, draining them, then simmering them for a further 1–2 hours.

Method

Mix all the ingredients and stand for 1 hour before serving. A variation is to add aduki or black eyed beans for interest and colour. (Remember to soak these first before cooking.)

This salad will keep 2–3 days in the fridge.

Rice salad

Ingredients for 6
6 oz (175 g)   Brown rice, cooked
2 oz (50 g)   Small button
mushrooms
1   Small red pepper (diced)
1   Small green pepper (diced)
1   Small red eating apple (diced
but not peeled)
Salt and pepper
Enough French dressing (p.10) to
coat the salad.

This useful salad is very flexible. It is based upon cooked rice, to which you can add vegetables of your choice. In the following recipe I suggest a selection of vegetables. But other vegetables you might use are: chopped celery, raw cauliflower florets, tinned sweetcorn, flageolet and other cooked beans, chopped onions, chives, sliced radish or chopped olives. You can also add nuts such as walnuts or peanuts, or use dill, parsley or mint. If you like a tangy flavour, add ½ teaspoon of mild curry. The salad can be served alone or with hard-boiled eggs, ham or spiced salt beef. Use lettuce and tomatoes to garnish.

If the rice is fresh the salad will keep several days in the fridge.

Mushroom salads

These salads are absolutely delicious. Mushrooms are available all year round and are consistently good. I prefer button mushrooms for salads but the large 'flats' are ideal for cooking.

Mushroom salad

Ingredients for 4–6
8 oz (225 g)   Button mushrooms
1 dessertspoon   Horseradish
sauce
2 tablespoons   Mayonnaise
1 dessertspoon   Fresh double
cream or sour cream
Salt and pepper

Method

Mushrooms don't need skinning or washing. Simply wipe them over with a cloth if they are a little dirty. The stalks are also used. Mix the dressing, season, fold in the mushrooms and allow to stand 1 hour before serving. If the flavour is strong add a little more cream.

25

Pickled mushrooms (1)

Ingredients
8 oz (225 g)   Button mushrooms
3 fl oz (75 ml)   White wine
vinegar
1 dessertspoon   Sugar
2 fl oz (50 ml)   Olive oil

Method

Mix the vinegar, sugar and olive oil. Toss mushrooms in the dressing and refrigerate for 24 hours to marinade. This is wonderful as a starter served with squares of crisp buttered toast.

Pickled mushrooms (2)

Ingredients
8 oz (225 g)   Button mushrooms
1 dessertspoon   Brown sugar
1 dessertspoon   Mixed dried
herbs
1 teaspoon   Worcester sauce
1 teaspoon   Horseradish sauce
2 teaspoons   French mustard
1 tablespoon   Olive oil
Enough basic dressing (p.10) to
coat

Method

Mix all the ingredients for the dressing together. Toss the mushrooms in the dressing and marinade for 24 hours.

All these salads will keep several days in the fridge.

Fresh potato salad

Ingredients for 4–6
2 lb (1 kilo)   Scrubbed potatoes
5 tablespoons   Homemade
mayonnaise (p.10)
1 tablespoon   Flaked dried onion
Salt and pepper
Fresh chopped mint (optional)

This is a very basic salad that can be served hot or cold. It is delicious with cold meats such as chicken or turkey. It is especially good with smoked mackerel. I like using flaked dried onions. They give a crispness to the salad and leave no after-taste.

Method

Scrub the potatoes with a plastic scouring pad, and cover with cold water. Bring to the boil, cover and simmer for 10 minutes or until tender. Don't overcook. Tip out the hot water and fill with cold water to cool them. I keep the skins on the potatoes but if preferred you may skin them easily at this stage. Cut into 1-inch cubes. Season with salt and pepper. Stir in mayonnaise, dry onions and chopped mint. Chopped red and green peppers make a colourful addition.

This keeps 2–3 days in the fridge.

Red cabbage salad

Ingredients for 6–8
1 lb (450 g)   Red cabbage
2   Green eating apples (diced)
Enough basic dressing (p.10) to coat
Salt and pepper

This is a tasty colourful salad. It must be dressed after shredding as cabbage turns brown when left. It is best prepared a day before use.

Method

Slice the cabbage and apples very finely or grate it coarsely in the food processor. Add the dressing and refrigerate over 24 hours. Chopped celery makes an interesting addition.

This will keep several days in the fridge.

Carrot and orange salad

Ingredients for 4–6
1 lb (450 g)   Carrots
Juice of 1 large orange
1 dessertspoon   Demerara sugar
2 oz (50 g)   Sultanas

This is a delicious colourful salad, full of vitamins and available all year round. It is a staple salad in Israel.

Method

If the carrots are young and clean just give them a wipe and top and tail them, otherwise peel them first. Grate them finely on a grater or coarsely in the food processor. Mix all the ingredients together.

This only keeps 24 hours even if refrigerated because the juice ferments quickly.

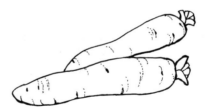

Piquant carrot salad

Ingredients for 4–6
1 lb (450 g)   Carrots
2 tablespoons   Lemon juice
4 tablespoons   Olive oil
3 cloves   Crushed garlic
1   Small onion
1 heaped teaspoon   Cumin
Salt and pepper

This is a favourite Middle Eastern dish. It is delicious mixed with chopped tomato and cucumber.

Method

Peel, clean and grate the carrot and onion finely. Mix together the oil, lemon juice, crushed garlic, cumin, salt and pepper. Mix well and add to the carrot and onion.

This will keep a couple of days in the fridge.

Tomato salad

Ingredients for 4–6
2 lb (1 kilo)   Hard ripe tomatoes
5 fl oz (150 ml)   Carton sour cream
1 dessertspoon   Dried onions
Salt and pepper
Chopped parsley to decorate

This salad is another Israeli staple, especially favoured on the kibbutz. It is particularly good when the tomatoes have been freshly picked and have their strongest scent and flavour.

Method

Wipe and cut the tomatoes in quarters. Add the sour cream, dried onion, salt and pepper. Decorate with chopped parsley.

Traditional Coleslaw

Ingredients for 4–6
1 lb (450 g)   Hard white cabbage
2 Medium-sized   Carrots, peeled, top and tailed
1 large or 1 small onion according to taste
2–3 tablespoons   Homemade mayonnaise (p.10)
Salt and pepper

Everyone likes this salad, so it's a good standby – especially since hard white cabbage is available all year.

Method

Slice the cabbage very thinly or use the coarse grater in the food processor. Grate the carrot and the onion. Mix all the ingredients together, adding more mayonnaise if wished. Season and refrigerate until needed.

Celeriac salad

Ingredients for 4–6
1 lb (450 g)   Celeriac root
2 tablespoons   Mayonnaise
1 tablespoon   Sour cream
1 teaspoon   French mustard
Salt and pepper

Celeriac is a versatile root vegetable which has a delicious herby smell of celery. It is excellent as a salad or as a flavouring for stews, casseroles and soups.

Method

Mix the mayonnaise, cream and mustard. Peel and grate the celeriac. Dress the celeriac before it turns brown. Season with salt and pepper.

This salad will keep for 2 days in the fridge.

Bulgar wheat salad

Ingredients for 4–6
4 oz (125 g)   Dry bulgar wheat
Juice of 1 lemon
2 cloves   Crushed garlic
3–4   Chopped spring onions
2 tablespoons   Olive oil
2   Tomatoes cut into small cubes
2 oz (50 g)   Chopped fresh parsley
1   Small green pepper (finely chopped)
Salt and pepper

This salad served with cubes of feta or cheddar cheese and a few stuffed olives is a meal in itself.

Method

Pour boiling water onto the bulgar wheat in a big bowl. Allow it to stand for 30 minutes. Add the rest of the prepared ingredients and stand for 2–3 hours.

This will keep 2 3 days in the fridge.

Vegetable side dishes

Sweet sour cabbage

Ingredients for 6
1 lb (450 g)   Hard white cabbage
2 tablespoons   White sugar
Juice of 1 lemon
Salt and pepper

This is an absolutely delicious dish from a very ordinary vegetable.

Method

Thinly slice the cabbage. Put it in a saucepan and bring to the boil in an inch of water. Simmer for 10 minutes covered with a tight lid. Lightly chop the cabbage, drain off any excess water and add the lemon juice, sugar, salt and pepper to taste. The amount of sugar and lemon can be altered to suit your own taste.

This will keep for 24 hours, but it is better to make it fresh each time.

Potato latkes or fritters

This makes a delicious filling dish on its own accompanied by a dessertspoon of sour cream and apple purée. It is also good with grated cheddar on the top. Instead of potato, you could use grated carrot, grated cooked beet, grated apple, or grated courgette and apple. A mixture of potato and

Ingredients for 4
1 lb (450 g)   Potatoes
2   Eggs
1   Large onion
Salt and pepper
2 tablespoons   Medium matza
meal (or flour or breadcrumbs)
Oil for frying

cottage cheese is also very appetising. It is a very versatile recipe. Garnish with sprigs of parsley.

Method

Wash the potatoes and, if the skins are good, grate the whole on a fine grater. Add the grated onion, eggs, seasoning and finally the matza meal. Then heat a little oil in a frying pan and spoon the mixture into the pan allowing 2 heaped dessert-spoons of mixture per fritter. Fry until golden brown on both sides, then turn the heat down to cook through for a further 5 minutes. Turn onto kitchen roll to drain. Serve.

These keep 2–3 days in the fridge and freeze very well with greaseproof paper between each one.

 # Baked sweet potato or yams

Ingredients for 2–4
1 lb (450 g)   Sweet potato or yam
(best to buy the largest)
1 oz (25 g)   Butter
Salt and pepper
Chopped fresh herbs (optional)

I have added this to my recipe book because the sweet potato or yam is now available in supermarkets. They can be used instead of, or with, baked or roast potatoes for Sunday lunch. The colour ranges from white to deep carrot orange. Garnished with a knob of butter and seasoning they are very good indeed. Of course they can be boiled as well, but this is by far the tastiest method of cooking them.

Method

Scrub the potato, prick with a fork several times. Put into a hot oven and lay on the oven rack. Allow to cook until soft. It may take ½–1 hour. Cut lengthwise and decorate with butter, salt and pepper and fresh herbs.

These will keep for 24 hours only.

Tyneside fried leeks

Ingredients for 4
1 lb (450 g)   Leeks
4 oz (125 g)   Margarine (oil or butter can be used)
Salt and pepper

This is a warming high-caloried dish. It is very good with Sunday lunch or as a snack with a cheese omelette and tomatoes.

Method

Wash the leeks. Cut into 1-inch lengths and dry with a towel. Drop the leeks into hot fat in the frying pan. Fry on a high heat for 5 minutes turning all the time, season. Then lower the heat and continue to cook the leeks until they are limp and cooked. The smell is wonderful.

The cooked leeks will keep several days in the fridge.

Fennel in white sauce

Ingredients for 4
1 lb (450 g)   Fennel (1 large bulb)
1 oz (25 g)   Margarine
1 oz (25 g)   Flour
½ pint (300 ml)   Milk
Dill, parsley or a little grated cheese for sauce.

Fennel has a very delicate flavour so the sauce must be very mild to complement it. This is a very filling dish.

Method

Trim some of the outer leaves and feathery bits off the fennel. Slice off the root. Rinse and cut into 4 quarters. Bring to the boil in 1 inch of seasoned water. Cover with a tight lid and simmer for 10 minutes. Test with a fork to see when it is soft. Meanwhile make the roux with the margarine, flour, milk and seasoning. Make the flavour of your choice by adding either chopped parsley, dill or a little grated cheese to the sauce. Put the fennel in an attractive serving dish, pour the sauce over and brown slightly under the grill. Serve.

This should be served immediately. If the fennel is kept separately, it will keep 2–3 days. The cooked fennel will also freeze.

Broccoli in cheese sauce

Ingredients for 4
1 lb (450 g)   Broccoli or calabrese
1 oz (25 g)   Margarine
1 oz (25 g)   Flour
½ pint (300 ml)   Milk
1 oz (25 g)   Grated cheese
Salt and pepper

You can use either broccoli or calabrese for this recipe. They are both tasty served alone but dressed in a cheese sauce they are delicious. Serve with fish and tomatoes.

Method

Rinse the broccoli. Cut off the woody ends and cut through the thick ends with a sharp knife. Bring to the boil in 1-inch of seasoned water. Then simmer using a tight-fitting lid for 10 minutes until tender. Meanwhile make the roux with the margarine, flour and milk (p.11). Add the cheese, season and pour over the broccoli. Put it under the grill for a few minutes to brown.

Make fresh each time.

String beans in tomato sauce

Ingredients for 4–6
1 lb (450 g)   Tin of beans (drained) – or use fresh string beans (topped and tailed)
4 oz (125 g)   Tomato purée
1 oz (25 g)   Margarine or butter
1 teaspoon   Sugar
Shake of worcester or tamari sauce
1 clove   Crushed garlic
Salt and pepper

This is a good way of dressing tinned or fresh beans.

Method

Cook the beans in a little salted water until tender. Drain, then mix the other ingredients together and add to the beans. Reheat and season if necessary.

This will keep in the fridge for 2 days.

_____
_____
_____
_____
_____
_____
_____
_____
_____

Jane's hot dutch brown beans

Ingredients for 4–6
½ lb (250 g)   Dutch brown beans
1 large tablespoon   Honey
1 oz (25 g)   Butter
Salt and pepper

This can be served as a starter or as a side dish to a vegetarian or meat meal. You must plan 2 days in advance.

Method

Soak the beans in water for 24–48 hours. Drain and recover with water. Bring to the boil in a covered saucepan and simmer for 1–2 hours until tender. Then continue on a very low heat with the lid off until the water is reduced to a thick sauce. Add the honey, seasoning and butter.

This will keep 2 days in the fridge.

Egyptian foule beans

Ingredients for 4–6
1 lb (450 g)   Egyptian foule
beans or 1½ lb (750 g) fresh
broad beans
1 tablespoon   Olive oil
1 tablespoon   Lemon Juice
2 cloves   Crushed garlic
1   Large diced tomato
1 tablespoon   Tahini paste
Salt and pepper

This bean is a staple in Egypt and is served in glasses on the streets of Cairo. It is good served with wholemeal bread and butter.

Method

If using tinned beans simply mix all the ingredients, incorporating the liquid. If using broad beans, shell and cook them first in a little water until tender. Drain, reserving ½ cup of the cooking liquid. Add this and the beans to remaining ingredients. Reheat and serve.

This is best freshly made.

Main courses
Bean dishes

Soya bean loaf

Ingredients for 6
6 oz (175 g)   Soya beans (soaked for 24 hours)
1–2 cloves   Garlic
1   Large onion (chopped)
4 sticks   Celery (chopped)
2   Tomatoes (skinned, peeled and chopped)
2 tablespoons   Tomato purée
4 oz (125 g)   Breadcrumbs or matza meal
4 tablespoons   Parsley (chopped)
1 teaspoon   Dry thyme
1   Egg
Salt and pepper
Oil for frying

Ingredients
1   Large onion (chopped and fried until transparent)
1 oz (25 g)   Margarine
1 oz (25 g)   Flour
½ pint (300 ml)   Milk
Salt and pepper

This can be served hot with hot side dishes or cold with cold salads, using mayonnaise as a dressing.

Method

Fry the chopped onions, garlic and celery until tender. Add the tomatoes and the purée. Cook for a further 5 minutes. Simmer the beans until soft. Drain off the water. Mash and stir them into the mixture. Add the matza meal, herbs, egg, salt and pepper. Grease a small loaf tin and line it with grease proof paper. Add the mixture and cover with grease proof paper to stop burning. Bake for 1 hour at regulo 5 (190°C). Cool a little before turning out. Serve it in slices with onion sauce.

The Sauce

Method

Make a roux (p.11). Add the onion, salt and pepper. Pour over the slices of soya loaf.

Lentil croquettes

This is an interesting mixture.

Ingredients for 6
8 oz (225 g)   Red lentils
2 tablespoons   Peanut butter
1 oz (25 g)   Chopped parsley
1 dessertspoon   Lemon juice
1   Egg
1 oz (25 g)   Matza meal
1 teaspoon   Marmite or yeast extract
2 oz (50 g)   Grated cheddar
Salt and pepper
Oil for frying

Method

Cover the lentils with water, bring to the boil and simmer for 20 minutes or until tender. Drain. Mix the peanut butter, lemon juice, marmite or yeast extract together with a little water. Add the rest of the ingredients. Mould the mixture into balls the size of a small egg. Dip them in flour and deep fry until golden. Drain on kitchen paper. Serve with parsley sauce and salad.

The Sauce

Ingredients
1 oz (25 g)   Chopped parsley
1 oz (25 g)   Margarine
1 oz (25 g)   Flour
½ pint (300 ml)   Milk
Salt and pepper

Method

Make a roux (p.11). Add the seasoning and the chopped parsley. Pour over the croquettes.

√Leek and cheddar flan

This is as good cold as hot.

Ingredients for 4–6
1½ lb (700 g)   Leeks
2   Eggs
½ pint (300 ml)   Milk
4 oz (125 g)   Grated cheddar cheese
1   Large Onion
Salt and pepper
8 oz (225 g)   Prepared shortcrust pastry (p.9)
1 dessertspoon   Soy sauce
1 teaspoon   Dried basil

Method

Slit the leeks from top to bottom and rinse, trim and cut into 2-inch lengths. Put into boiling salted water for just 5 minutes. Line an 8-inch flan ring with the pastry. Reinforce the inner edge with a snake of pastry. Prick the bottom. Layer the drained leeks with the cheese. Beat the eggs, add the milk, seasoning, and soy sauce, pour into the flan. Reserve some cheese for the top and sprinkle the herbs over it. Bake at regulo 8 (230°C) for 10 minutes to crisp the pastry. Then reduce the heat to regulo 5 (190°C) for a further 20 minutes until set and brown.

This keeps well in the fridge for several days and freezes well.

Pastry dishes
Aubergine flan or bake

Ingredients for 4–6
1 lb (450 g)   Aubergines
8 oz (225 g)   Potatoes (parboiled for 5 to 10 minutes and sliced)
5 oz (150 g)   Red kidney beans (pre-cooked or tinned)
*5 oz (150 g)   White kidney beans (pre-cooked or tinned)
3   Eggs
½ pint (300 ml)   Milk
1 oz (25 g)   Grated cheese to garnish
Salt and pepper
8 oz (225 g)   Prepared shortcrust pastry (p.9)

*NB. It is important that kidney beans are boiled for the first 15 minutes of the cooking time and then simmered for approx. 1¼ hours.

This is a tasty meal which is well balanced with protein. Served with salads it is quite filling. It can be made either in a pastry case or without the pastry in a pyrex high-sided dish. To spice up the dish, spread some tomato chutney over the potato layer.

Method

Slice and salt the aubergine for 1 hour to remove the bitterness. Rinse. Put the slices in a pan with an inch of water. Bring to the boil cover with a tight lid and simmer for 5 minutes. Meanwhile make the pastry (p.9). Line an 8–10 inch flan case. Prick the base. Layer the sliced aubergine, sliced potatoes, seasoning, beans and finally the seasoned egg and milk mixture. Garnish with grated cheese. Bake at regulo 8 (230°C) for 15 minutes. This crisps the pastry. Reduce the heat to regulo 4 (180°C) for a further 30 minutes to set the custard. This same mixture can be cooked in an ovenproof dish without the pastry. Garnish with sliced tomatoes and parsley sprigs.

Sweetcorn flan

Ingredients for 4–6
½ lb (225 g)   Prepared shortcrust pastry (p.9)
1 lb (450 g)   Tin of Canadian sweetcorn
2   Eggs
½ pint (300 ml)   Milk
2 oz (50 g)   Matza meal
½   Red pepper (chopped)
½   Green pepper (chopped)
Salt and pepper

This is especially nice for a buffet supper as it is good hot or cold. This dish was created in the restaurant.

Method

Line an 8-inch flan ring with rolled pastry – prick the bottom. It is a good idea to line the bottom edge of the flan with a thin sausage of pastry and press well in to stop leakage during cooking. Beat the eggs, add the milk and the corn puréed in the blender (reserve a few whole niblets for decoration). Add the matza meal and allow to stand for

10 minutes to enable the meal to swell. Season and stir. Pour into the pastry case. Cook at regulo 8 (230°C) for 10 minutes then regulo 4 for 20 minutes or until set. 10 minutes before the end of cooking sprinkle on the remaining corn and the chopped peppers.

This freezes well and keeps in the fridge several days.

Boracas
(spinach and egg in puff pastry)

Ingredients for 4
1 lb (450 g)   Cooked spinach (or tin drained leaf spinach)
4   Eggs
4 fl oz (100 ml)   Milk
5 oz (150 g)   Carton of cottage cheese or grated cheddar
4 cloves   Crushed garlic
8 oz (225 g)   Pack of puff pastry
1 oz (25 g)   Margarine
Salt and pepper

This is a very delicious and colourful meal which is full of nutrients. It is best served with salads. A favourite in the Middle East.

Method

Beat the eggs, add the milk, seasoning and pour into a pan with the melted margarine. Scramble the eggs over a low heat. Take the pan off the heat and stir in the cheese and crushed garlic. Roll out the pastry. Cut into 4 squares. Brush the edges with milk. Divide the egg mix and spinach into 4. Layer spinach and cooled egg mix on the pastry. Fold the pastry to form a triangle and seal the edges. Crimp the edges with a fork or with the fingers. Paint the surface with egg or milk and prick the top. Bake at regulo 7 or 220°C for 10 minutes then reduce heat to regulo 6 for 5–10 minutes. Take care not to burn. Serve straight away.

These will keep for 2–3 days and will reheat. They will also freeze but are far nicer served freshly made.

Bean and cheese loaf

Ingredients for 4–6
8 oz (225 g)   Self-raising flour
2 oz (50 g)   Margarine
1 oz (25 g)   Chopped nuts
4 oz (125 g)   Tinned borlotti beans (rinsed)
4 oz (125 g)   Tinned red kidney beans (rinsed)
4 oz (125 g)   Tinned chick peas (rinsed)
¼ pint (150 ml)   Milk
1   Egg
5 oz (150 g)   Grated cheddar cheese
Salt and pepper

Ingredients
4 oz (150 g)   Tin of tomato purée
1 oz (25 g)   Grated cheddar cheese
1–3 tablespoons   Single cream

This, served sliced with tomato and cream topping and warmed under the grill makes a delicious meal. Strangely enough, one or two minutes in the microwave to reheat the cut slices with topping improves the texture enormously.

Method

Rub the margarine into the flour. Add salt and pepper. Stir in the cheese, nuts and beans. Beat the egg and mix with the milk. Add to the dry ingredients and mix well. Turn into a tin lined with greaseproof paper and bake at regulo 4 (180°C) for 45–50 minutes. Cool a little before turning out. Slice and serve with salads.

Topping

Method

Mix and spoon over the slices. Reheat in the microwave or under a warm grill.

The bean loaves can keep up to a week in the fridge. The topping will keep 2–3 days in the fridge but will not freeze. The loaves will freeze well in a plastic bag. Remove the air and seal.

Stuffed cabbage encroûte

Ingredients for 6
2 lb (1 kilo)   White cabbage
8 oz (225 g)   Chopped dried apricots
2   Large onions
2 oz (50 g)   Flaked almonds
2 oz (50 g)   Halved walnuts
4 oz (125 g)   Sultanas
2 oz (50 g)   Halved cooked chestnuts
4 oz (100 g)   Mushrooms
1 tablespoon   Soy sauce
2 oz (50 g)   Ground almonds
8 oz (225 g)   Cooked bulgar wheat or rice
1 lb   Prepared puff pastry
Salt and pepper
Beaten egg
Oil to fry

Encroûte is a French term for baking a meal encased in pastry (usually puff pastry). This dish makes a marvellous show at a dinner party.

Method

Peel the cabbage. Make an incision near the root and peel from there. Drop the leaves in boiling water until limp. Cook the apricots in 2 cups of water. Fry the onions, add the chestnuts, almonds, sultanas, mushrooms and walnuts. Add the cooked apricots, ground almonds, rice or bulgar wheat and soy sauce to the frying pan. Lay the drained cabbage leaves flat and spoon the mixture over. Fold into parcels. Roll out the pastry as thinly as possible. Put it on a large baking sheet. Build the parcels in the middle. Paint the edges of the pastry with beaten egg and fold the pastry together. Crimp the edges with your fingers. Paint the whole with beaten egg. Prick the surface with a fork. Bake at regulo 8 for 10 minutes then turn down to regulo 6 (200°C) for about 20–30 minutes until it is golden brown. Serve with sour cream and mango chutney. Roast potatoes and buttered carrots would make a colourful addition.

This is best to eat at once but will be fine the next day.

Vegetable dishes

Potato and apple bake

Ingredients for 4–6
1½ lb (700 g)   Potatoes
(parboiled for 5–10 minutes with
skins on)
1½ lb (700 g)   Large cooking
apples (bramleys are excellent)
4 oz (125 g)   Grated cheddar
cheese
2   Beaten eggs
5 fl oz (150 ml)   Milk
2 oz (50 g)   Dried breadcrumbs
1 oz (25 g)   Margarine
Salt and pepper
Paprika powder

This is another created at the restaurant which has become very popular.

Method

Cut the cooking apples into thick slices leaving the skin on. Place a layer in the bottom of a high-sided ovenproof dish. Cover with a layer of thickly-sliced potatoes. Spread a tablespoon of tomato relish on the potatoes and season. Sprinkle on some grated cheese. Repeat this until the apple and potatoes are finished. Leave some cheese to sprinkle on the top. Mix the egg and milk and pour over the layers. Finish with breadcrumbs, grated cheese, seasoning and a sprinkle of red paprika. Put knobs of margarine on the top and cover with foil. Take the foil off for the last 10 minutes of cooking to brown. Bake for 1 hour at regulo 6 (200°C). Serve with salad.

This will keep 2–3 days in the fridge and freezes well.

Vegetarian stew

Ingredients for 4–6
2 lb (1 kilo)   Mixed vegetables
(courgette, green beans, swede,
etc.)
8 oz (225 g)   Tin of plum
tomatoes
4 oz (125 g)   Tin of tomato purée
3 cloves   Crushed garlic
(optional)
4 oz (125 g)   Tinned red kidney
beans (washed)
4 oz (125 g)   Tinned white
kidney beans (washed)
2 oz (50 g)   Margarine
2   Bay leaves
1 dessertspoon   Soy sauce
Salt and pepper
1½ pints (900 ml)   Water

Any vegetable can go into the stew, apart from cauliflower, potato, cabbage and spinach since they tend to go mushy. Washed and drained beans are added to give texture and protein to the meal.

Method

Cut the vegetables into 1-inch pieces. Slice and fry the onion until transparent. Drop the rest of the prepared vegetables in the fat and fry for a few minutes turning constantly. Add 1½ pints of water and the rest of the ingredients. Bring to the boil, simmer for 30 minutes. Stirring occasionally, serve the stew on a bed of rice.

This will keep for a week in the fridge, tasting better as the flavours blend. It freezes very well.

Courgette and oat bake

Ingredients for 4–6
2   Large onions
1 lb (450 g)   Courgettes
14 oz (400 g)   Tin of tomatoes
1 dessertspoon   Dried mixed
herbs
4 tablespoons   Cooking oil
4 tablespoons   Rolled oats
4 oz (125 g)   Grated cheddar
cheese
4   Eggs
¼ pint (150 ml)   Vegetable stock
or yeast extract
Salt and pepper

This again is a substantial meal, very popular in the restaurant. Since courgettes are available almost always, it can be made all year round.

Method

Slice and fry the onions in tablespoons oil until transparent. Add the rolled oats and cook for 3 minutes. Add the stock, and cook until it thickens stirring all the time. Fry the sliced courgettes in the remaining oil, place in a shallow oven dish, season and cover with the tomatoes and herbs. Beat the eggs and add them to the oat mixture. Stir in ¾ of the cheese and pour the mixture over the vegetables. Sprinkle the remaining cheese on the top. Bake at regulo 5 (190°C) for 30 minutes. Check that it is done by sliding a knife in the centre. It should come out cleanly.

This will keep well in the fridge for a few days. It reheats in the oven or a microwave oven. It also freezes well.

Aubergine curry

Ingredients for 4–6

1½ lb (700 g)   Aubergines
½ lb (225 g)   Mushrooms
½ lb (225 g)   Mixed red and green peppers
1 Large tablespoon of tomato purée
2 oz (50 g)   Sultanas
1 Heaped tablespoon of mild madras curry
1 teaspoon   Turmeric
2 oz (50 g)   Flaked almonds
2 oz (50 g)   Margarine or 3 tablespoons of oil
½ lb (225 g)   Onions
3 cloves   Garlic
Salt and pepper
½ pint (300 ml)   Water

This is absolutely delicious. The strength of the curry can be varied by adding more or less curry powder. It is a very filling dish, especially when served on a bed of brown rice.

Method

Wipe and cut aubergines into 1-inch cubes. Fry the onion until transparent. Add the aubergine and peppers, curry powder, turmeric, garlic and seasoning, toss the vegetables around in the hot oil for a few minutes. Add the rest of the ingredients and ½ pint (300 ml) water. Bring to the boil, simmer with a tight lid for 20 minutes. Taste and reseason. Add more water if necessary and cook for a further 5 minutes. Serve.

Chick pea and lentil curry

Ingredients for 4–6

4 oz (125 g)   Chick peas (soaked overnight)
4 oz (125 g)   Green lentils (soaked overnight)
1 tablespoon   Oil
1   Large onion
8 oz (225 g)   Tin of plum tomatoes
1 tablespoon   Tomato purée
A shake of chilli sauce
1 teaspoon   Cumin
½ teaspoon   Ground coriander
1 teaspoon   Ground ginger
2   Cardamom seeds (shelled)
2 cloves   Crushed garlic
Salt and pepper

This contains a lot of different spices – but it's well worth the effort!

Method

Drain the chick peas and lentils. Cover with cold water, bring to the boil and simmer for 2 hours until tender. Fry the sliced onions in hot oil, add the spices and garlic and fry for a further 2 minutes. Add the chick peas and lentils together with the cooking water. Add the tomatoes and tomato purée. Simmer for a further 10 minutes. Serve on a bed of brown rice.

Pasta dishes

Spinach lasagne

Ingredients for 4–6
14–16 oz (400 g)   Drained
tinned spinach (or use fresh)
6 oz (175 g)   Lasagne
4 oz (100 g)   Cottage cheese
1   Egg
2 oz (50 g)   Mushrooms
2 oz (50 g)   Tomatoes, skinned
and chopped

The Sauce Ingredients
2 oz (50 g)   Grated cheese
1 oz (25 g)   Margarine
1 oz (25 g)   Flour
½ pint (300 ml)   Milk
Salt and pepper
Nutmeg (optional)

This meal is very good for a dinner party. It can be served with salads or hot vegetables. Use pre-cooked pasta – this saves a great deal of time.

Method

Add the cottage cheese and the egg to the drained spinach. Season. (If using tinned spinach season with pepper only as the spinach is usually tinned in brine.) Place a layer of pasta at the bottom of a fire proof dish, followed by a layer of spinach mixture and a further layer of pasta. Cover with the chopped tomatoes and sliced mushrooms. Season. Top with a further layer of pasta.

The Sauce

Make a sauce as shown on page (p.11) Add the grated cheese and pour over the lasagne. Sprinkle with nutmeg. Cook at regulo 3 (160°C) for 40 minutes. If not browned at the end of cooking raise the temperature to regulo 6 (200°C) for 5–10 minutes.

_____
_____
_____
_____
_____
_____
_____
_____
_____
_____
_____
_____
_____
_____

Savoury egg noodle

Ingredients for 4–6
8 oz (225 g) Egg noodles
1 Small yellow pepper
1 Small red pepper
1 Small green pepper
1 oz (25 g) Capers in brine (drained)
1 lb (450 g) Aubergine (diced)
1 oz (25 g) Sultanas
1 oz (25 g) Stuffed olives
Salt and pepper
3 cloves Crushed garlic
2 tablespoons Cooking oil
1 teaspoon Soy sauce

A tasty pasta dish to be served hot with salads. It's also tasty with seasoned and buttered jacket potatoes.

Method

Cook the noodles as directed on the packet. Drain and season. Simmer the aubergine for 10 minutes until tender in a little water. Season. Cut the peppers into 1-inch pieces and fry in the oil with the crushed garlic. Add the drained aubergine. Add the capers, olive, sultanas, soy sauce and noodles. Taste and season. Serve in an oven dish, and keep warm in the oven until ready to serve.

This keeps 2–3 days in the fridge. It also freezes well.

✓ Kings Pantry pizza

Ingredients for 4–6

The bread
8 oz (225 g) Wholemeal flour
1 teaspoon Salt
1 teaspoon Sugar
½ oz (12 g) Fresh yeast
½ cup Warmed milk
2 Eggs
2 oz (50 g) Warm creamed butter

The topping
1 lb (450 g) Fresh tomatoes (quartered)
1 lb (450 g) onions (finely sliced)
4 oz (100 g) Grated cheddar cheese
4 oz (100 g) Sliced mushrooms
1 dessertspoon Dried mixed herbs
1 dessertspoon Oregano
Salt and pepper
Oil for frying

This is our staple which has been served since the opening of the restaurant. I use a wholemeal bread base.

Method

To make the bread, put the flour in a deep warmed bowl. Mix the yeast, sugar, salt and milk together. Add this to the flour together with the beaten eggs. Work the creamed butter into the mix. Cover and leave to rise for 40 minutes in a warm place. Flour the dough and roll to the size of a large baking sheet and prove again in the warm oven for 10 minutes.

To make the topping, fry the onions in the oil until transparent. Add the mushrooms and tomatoes and toss in the oil. Season and add the herbs. Spread the mixture over the dough and sprinkle on the grated cheese. Bake at regulo 6 (200°C) for 20–30 minutes. Serve immediately accompanied by mixed salads.

Desserts

Muesli yoghurt

Ingredients for 2
5 fl oz (150 ml)   Carton of plain yoghurt
2–3 dessertspoons of muesli
1 teaspoon   Demerara sugar
1 teaspoon   Honey
Flaked almonds to decorate
Glacé cherry
Whipped cream to decorate

This refreshing dessert is popular at parties. It's even good for breakfast.

Method

Mix the yoghurt, muesli, sugar and honey together. Serve in long glasses and decorate with flaked almonds, a glacé cherry and some whipped cream.

Make fresh as needed as the muesli swells over a period of time making the dessert too thick and heavy.

Melon and ginger

Ingredients for 4
2 small or 1 medium ripe melon
1 small jar of stem ginger
A little whipped cream (optional)
Angelica
Glacé cherries

This can be served as a dessert or a starter. I prefer to eat it at the end of the meal. Small ripe ogen or honeydew melons are suitable.

Method

Cut the melons into 2 or 4 pieces, remove seeds. Run a knife between the skin and the fruit and cut the fruit into slices. Drip the syrup from the stem ginger on to the melon and add the chopped stem ginger. Leave to marinade. Decorate with glacé cherries and angelica. Chill before serving.

Make as needed.

Banana split

Ingredients for 4
4   Ripe bananas
2 oz (50 g)   Chopped nuts
1 tablespoons   Clear honey
8 oz (225 g)   Green and black grapes
Juice of 1 lemon
8 scoops of vanilla ice cream
5 fl oz (140 ml)   Carton of whipping cream
Ice cream sauce and chopped nuts to decorate

This is a Kings Pantry treat. It is a great favourite with the children, best served in long flat dishes.

Method

Slice the banana lengthways and lay in a flat dish. Mix the nuts and the honey and place a teaspoon of this mixture at each end of the banana. Squeeze lemon juice over the banana. Wash the grapes and place them around each banana. Top with 2 scoops of ice cream and whipped cream. Decorate with ice cream sauces and chopped nuts.

Make as needed.

Knickerbocker glory

Ingredients for 4
12   Boudoir biscuits
1 lb (450 g)   Fresh fruit in fruit juice (bananas, raspberries, apples, etc.)
4 scoops of ice cream
5 fl oz (140 ml)   Carton of whipped cream
Ice cream sauce and glacé cherries to decorate

This old-fashioned party dish is a favourite in the summer. You need long glasses and spoons to serve this properly.

Method

Break 2 boudoir biscuits into each glass. Fill up to three-quarters with the fresh fruit. Top with a scoop of ice cream and finally with whipped cream. Decorate with ice cream sauce and a glacé cherry. Finally, finish by inserting another boudoir biscuit and a long spoon into the glass.

Make as needed.

Apple fritters

Ingredients for 4
4 oz (125 g)   Flour
1   Beaten egg
¼ pint (150 ml)   Milk
Pinch of salt
1 lb (450 g)   Very large cooking apples (Bramleys if possible)
Sugar for dusting
Oil for frying

These are absolutely delicious but they must be served immediately. Bananas, or sliced pineapples also make excellent fritters. Serve with sour or fresh whipped cream and maple syrup.

Method

Sieve flour and salt into bowl. Beat in egg. Gradually beat in milk. Cut the apples into thick rings and take out the core. Don't peel. Pat them dry with a cloth. Heat the oil in a frying pan. Dip the apple rings in the batter. Fry gently on each side until golden. Dust with sugar and keep warm. Serve with sour cream, fresh whipped cream or yoghurt and maple syrup.

Make fresh each time.

American pancakes

Ingredients for 4
8 oz (225 g)   Self-raising flour
2 oz (50 g)   Sugar
2   Eggs (beaten)
½ pint (300 ml)   Milk
1 tablespoon   Powdered milk
Oil for frying

Unlike British pancakes, these are made with self-raising flour and have a spongy texture. In America they are generally served stacked with fresh fruit and maple syrup and eaten at breakfast. They can be topped with sour cream, fresh cream or yoghurt. Alternatively, they can be served with lemon juice, butter and sugar and accompanied by spices such as cinnamon. For savoury pancakes, sprinkle them with grated cheese and serve with a knob of butter.

Method

Slowly add the milk and powdered milk to flour beating together with a whisk. Add the eggs, and sugar and beat well. Pour a little oil in a frying pan and heat. Ladle 2 tablespoons of batter into the pan and fry gently, turning the pancake when the surface is covered in bubbles. Stack the pancakes and keep hot. To make savoury pancakes, leave out the sugar and add ½ teaspoon salt.

These will keep well in the fridge for 2–3 days and freeze well.

Kings Pantry trifle

Ingredients for 4
Some stale cake
1 packet   Strawberry jelly
4 oz (125 g)   Frozen or fresh
strawberries (or raspberries)
½ pint (300 ml)   Thick custard
A little whipped cream
Chopped nuts
1 fl oz (25 ml)   Sherry (optional)

This is a good way of using up leftover cake. It's always popular with children and also with adults if there is a little alcohol in it!

Method

Break the cake into small pieces, and quarter-fill 4 long glasses with it. Divide the sherry between the 4 glasses. Make the jelly according to the directions on the packet and pour it over the cake, till the glasses are half full. Drop in a dessertspoon of fruit. When the jelly has set add the custard leaving about an inch at the top. Chill until ready to serve. Top with whipped cream and chopped nuts.

Apricot or prune whip

Ingredients for 4–6
4 oz (125 g)   Dried apricots or
prunes (stones removed)
1   Apricot flavour jelly
8 fl oz (200 ml)   Tin of
evaporated milk
5 fl oz (150 ml)   Whipped cream
Roasted almonds

This is a simple, but tasty dish. It can be dressed up with whipped cream and chopped nuts.

Method

Cover the fruit with water and simmer for 20 minutes. Blend until smooth. Meanwhile dissolve the jelly in ¼ of the water recommended in the directions on the packet. Add to the fruit together with the tin of evaporated milk. Mix and pour into long glasses. Set in the fridge. Serve with whipped cream and nuts.

Apple pie and spiced apple dessert

Ingredients for 4–6
1 lb (450 g)   Prepared shortcrust
pastry
2 lb (1 kilo)   Cooking apples
(Bramleys)
2 oz (50 g)   Sultanas
1 teaspoon   Cinnamon
1 teaspoon   Mixed spice
2–4 oz (50–100 g)   Demerara
sugar according to taste
1 oz (25 g)   Butter
2 tablespoons   Medium matza
meal (for pie only)
Juice of 1 lemon

This is a recipe I prepared years ago for the family. It is very good. It can be served either with or without a pastry case.

Method

Peel and slice the apples. Cook in ½ cup of water together with the sultanas, butter, sugar, lemon juice and spices (about 5–10 minutes). If making the pie, add the matza meal. This absorbs the liquid so that it does not ruin the pastry in the pie. Prepare the pastry (p.9). Roll out and line a pie or flan dish. Prick the base. Fill with the apple mixture. Brush the edges of the pastry and cover with a pastry lid. Seal. Brush the top of the pie. Prick with a fork and sprinkle with a little brown sugar. Bake at regulo 8 (230°C) for 10 minutes to crisp the pastry. Continue for a further 20 minutes at regulo 5 (190°C). Cool a little before serving. Serve with whipped cream and or vanilla ice cream. This is delicious hot or cold.

This will keep several days in the fridge and freezes well.

Cakes and biscuits

Orange liqueur cake

Ingredients for 6
2 Eggs
8 oz (225 g)   Self-raising flour
6 oz (175 g)   White sugar
½ pint (300 ml)   Milk

Syrup
Juice of 2 oranges
2 oz (50 g)   Sugar
1 wine glass liqueur (apricot or rum are excellent)
Small wine glass or liqueur glas   Liqueur

This is a lovely special cake, but must be served fresh. There is no fat in the cake so it must be eaten quickly or it will become dry.

Method

Place flour and sugar in bowl. Gradually stir in beaten egg and milk to make a thick batter. Pour into a greased and lined, round or square cake tin, bake at regulo 4 (180°C) for 20 minutes until golden brown. Cool. Turn the cake out and remove paper. Return to the tin upside down. Prepare the syrup by combining the ingredients in a saucepan and bringing to the boil. Stir to dissolve the sugar. Pour carefully over the cake. Cool and serve with whipped cream.

Banana bread

Ingredients for 6–8
3   Ripe bananas
2 tablespoons   Milk
1 teaspoon   Bicarbonate of soda
6 oz (175 g)   Self-raising flour
4 oz (125 g)   Margarine
2   Eggs
4 oz (125 g)   White sugar

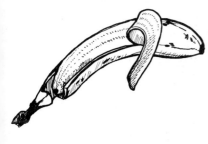

This is an excellent cake to serve with coffee. The bananas give a moist texture. Over ripe bananas unsuitable for eating are excellent since they are usually cheap and produce a good strong flavour.

Method

Mash the bananas well. Add the milk and mix. Melt the margarine and pour it over the flour, soda and sugar, mix well. Beat in the eggs. Add the mashed banana and mix again. Grease and line a loaf tin with greaseproof paper and fill with the mixture. Bake at regulo 4 (180°C) for 30–40 minutes until golden brown.

This keeps well for a few days (best in the fridge). It freezes well.

Carrot cake with cream cheese topping

Ingredients for 8–10
8 fl oz (225 ml)   Cooking oil
12 oz (325 g)   Sugar
4   Eggs
1 teaspoon   Vanilla essence
1 lb (450 g)   Freshly grated carrots
8 oz (225 g)   Plain flour
1 teaspoon   Mixed spice
1 tablespoon   Baking powder
2 oz (50 g)   Sultanas
2 oz (50 g)   Chopped nuts (optional)

Topping

Ingredients
4 oz (125 g)   Cream cheese
5 fl oz (150 ml)   Carton sour cream
Juice of 1 or 2 lemons
2 oz (50 g)   Granulated sugar

This recipe was brought back from New York by my daughter Sharon. I have adapted it to our use and created a simple topping to serve with it.

Method

Mix together the oil and sugar. Add the eggs and vanilla essence. Mix well. Add the grated carrot, flour, spice, baking powder, sultanas and nuts. Mix together well. Line a round or square tin with greaseproof paper. Fill the tin and bake at regulo 4 (180°C) for 40 minutes until golden brown. Check with a knife to see that it is well done in the centre.

Method

Mix the ingredients adding as much lemon as you wish. Spread over the cooled cake.

Fatless strawberry yoghurt cake

Ingredients for 6–8
6 oz (175 g)   Wholemeal flour
1 teaspoon   Baking powder
½ teaspoon   Bicarbonate of soda
Pinch of salt
8 oz (225 ml)   Strawberry yoghurt
3   Eggs
6 oz (175 g)   White sugar
1 teaspoon   Grated lemon rind
1 teaspoon   Strawberry flavouring

This has a delicious yoghurt flavour.

Method

Mix all the dry ingredients except the sugar together – whisk the eggs with the sugar until thick enough to trail. Add the lemon rind, strawberry flavouring and yoghurt. Then mix all the ingredients together gently. Line a cake tin with greaseproof paper. Grease the paper. Bake for 35–45 minutes at regulo 4 (180°C). Cool for 5 minutes before turning out.

This keeps moist for several days and freezes well.

Poppyseed cake

Ingredients for 8–10
4 oz (225 g)   Margarine
6 oz (175 g)   Sugar
3   Eggs
6 oz (175 g)   Plain flour
½ teaspoon   Salt
Juice of ½ lemon
2 oz (50 g)   Poppy seeds
⅓ pint (250 ml)   Milk

Another Pantry favourite. Poppyseeds are quite expensive but it makes a pleasant change.

Method

Bring the poppyseeds to the boil in the milk. Then take off the heat and allow to stand for 20 minutes. Separate the eggs. Cream the yolks and whisk the whites until stiff. Cream the margarine and sugar until fluffy, beat in the egg yolks. Add the plain flour, baking powder and salt. Mix well. Folding the whisked egg whites. Mix well. Add the poppyseeds, milk and lemon juice. Grease a loaf tin. Fill with the mixture. Bake for 35–45 minutes at regulo 4 (180°C) until well done. Check with a knife to see that the centre is cooked.

This stays fresh several days and freezes well.

Muesli cake

Ingredients for 8–10
12 oz (325 g)   Muesli
8 oz (225 g)   Brown sugar
12 oz (325 g)   Sultanas
4 tablespoons   Malt extract
1 dessertspoon   Molasses
¾ pint (450 ml)   Apple juice

Place all ingredients in a stainless steel bowl and leave to soak for 2 days. After 2 days add the following ingredients:

4   Grated, unpeeled cooking apples
6 oz (175 g)   Wholemeal flour
6 oz (175 g)   Self-raising flour
3 dessertspoons   Baking powder

This has to be prepared 2–3 days in advance. It is a healthy filling vegan cake.

Method

Mix the ingredients well. Pack into a well-greased 10-inch cake tin. Bake at regulo 3 (160°C) for 1½–2 hours. Take care that it doesn't burn and that it is well cooked in the middle. Test the centre with a knife.

This will keep several days in an airtight tin and also freezes well.

Almond flan

Ingredients for 8
8 oz (225 g)   Prepared shortcrust pastry (p.9)
4 oz (125 g)   Margarine
4 oz (125 g)   White sugar
1 lb (450 g)   Cake crumbs
2 teaspoons   Almond essence
2 tablespoons   Cheap red jam
4   Eggs
1 oz (25 g)   Flaked almonds

This is my oldest recipe. It comes from wartime and uses old or damaged cake – obviously very useful when running a restaurant.

Method

Grease a fluted tart tin. Roll out the pastry and line the tin. Spread with the jam. Cream the margarine and the sugar. Beat in the 4 eggs and add the cake crumbs, and almond essence. Beat together. Fill the tart tin and top with flaked almonds. Bake at regulo 4 (180°C) for 30–40 minutes until golden.

This keeps well for a week and also freezes.

Refrigerated chocolate torte

Ingredients for 10
4 oz (125 g)   Margarine
2 oz (50 g)   Sugar
2 oz (50 g)   Cocoa powder (not drinking chocolate)
1½ dessertspoons   Golden syrup
4 oz (125 g)   Mixed dried fruit
1 oz (25 g)   Whole glacé cherries
1 teaspoon   Rum essence
1 oz (25 g)   Chopped nuts
4 oz (125 g)   Plain chocolate
Stale cake
Broken biscuits
Knob margarine

This was always popular at my children's birthday parties. There was never a crumb left.

Method

Melt the margarine, sugar, syrup and cocoa powder in a small pan. Add the fruit, cherries, rum essence, nuts and enough broken biscuits and stale cake to absorb all the moisture in the mixture. Press into a 10-inch well-greased, loose-bottomed cake tin. I use a potato masher to press the mixture down. Refrigerate for 1 hour. Melt the chocolate with knob margarine and pour it over the mixture.

This keeps well in a refrigerator in a plastic container. It also freezes well.

Date and apricot slices

Ingredients for 8–10
8 oz (225 g)   Wholemeal flour
8 oz (225 g)   Rolled oats
8 oz (225 g)   Margarine
3 oz (75 g)   Demerara sugar

Filling
10 oz (275 g)   Apricots or dates (dried)
Juice of 1 lemon
1 cup of water

These delicious vegan fruit slices are very appetising and filling. They have been a staple in the Pantry since we opened.

Method

Chop the fruit and simmer in a cup of water with the lemon juice for 10 minutes. Add more water if necessary to make the syrup the consistency of jam. Cool. Meanwhile, mix the flour and oats together. Rub in the margarine. Stir in the sugar, put half the mixture in an 8-inch square baking tray. Press down very well. Spread the fruit mixture on to the oats and cover the top with the rest of the oat mixture. Press down well with a potato masher. Bake at regulo 5 (190°C) for 35–40 minutes until golden on the top. Cut into squares while hot. Turn out when cool.

These keep well in a closed container and they also freeze.

Peanut macaroons

Ingredients for 4–6
2   Egg whites beaten
6 oz (175 g)   Sugar
6 oz (175 g)   Warmed peanut butter
Glacé cherries, or flaked almonds to decorate

Macaroons are usually made with almonds, but this nutty variety tastes just as good.

Method

Mix all the ingredients together. Put teaspoons of the mixture on rice paper on a baking tray leaving room for the mixture to spread. Decorate with a flaked almond or glacé cherry. Cook for 15 minutes at regulo 4 (180°C).

These will keep for a week in an airtight tin.

Rosemary biscuits

Ingredients for 6–8
12 oz (325 g)   Self-raising flour
8 oz (225 g)   Margarine
4 oz (125 g)   Sugar
1   Egg
1 dessertspoon   Fresh rosemary
¼ teaspoon   Salt

These are actually Rosemary's rosemary biscuits – perhaps this is an appropriate place to extend my thanks to Rosemary for helping me establish Kings Pantry.

Method

Rub the fat into the flour and add the sugar and rosemary. Bind together with the egg. Knead the mixture lightly. Roll it out and cut with a biscuit cutter. Place on a greased baking tray leaving room for the mixture to spread. Bake at regulo 5 (190°C) for 10 minutes. The biscuits will harden once out of the oven.

American brownies

Ingredients for 12
4 oz (125 g)   Cocoa (not drinking chocolate)
12 oz (325 g)   Margarine
12 oz (325 g)   Sugar
3   Eggs
6 oz (175 g)   Flour (half self-raising, half plain)
3 teaspoons   Vanilla essence
2 oz (50 g)   Chopped nuts (optional)

These are high-calorie chewy chocolate cookies that won't do your waistline any good but which taste wonderful. Care must be taken in cooking as they must be really soft when removed from the oven. They become harder once out.

Method

Mix all the dry ingredients together. Melt the margarine and pour into the mixture. Stir well. Do not beat. Pour into a well-greased tray so that the mixture is about ½-inch thick. Make sure it reaches the corners. Decorate with chopped nuts. Bake at regulo 4 (180°C) for 15–20 minutes. Test to see if they are cooked by pressing your thumb gently in the middle. It should leave an impression. Remove from the oven and mark into squares immediately. Don't turn them out until they are cool.

These keep well in an airtight tin and freeze well.

Health drinks

These drinks are very nourishing and slip down easily. Thus they are excellent in illness when appetites are poor, or during hot weather. They are also wonderful during pregnancy.

Banana and yoghurt

Ingredients for 2
1   Banana
1   Egg
5 fl oz (150 ml)   Carton plain yoghurt
1 teaspoon   Clear honey
Juice of ½ lemon
2 fl oz (50 ml)   Milk
1 teaspoon   Vanilla essence

This is really a meal in a glass. Serve it with a large straw.

Method

Blend and pour into tall glasses.

Blackcurrant and yoghurt

Ingredients for 2
½ cup of tinned blackcurrants or fresh if available
Juice of ½ lemon
5 fl oz (150 ml)   Yoghurt
3 fl oz (75 ml)   Milk
2   Eggs
2 teaspoons   Honey

Method

Blend well and taste. If it is too tart, add a little sugar. Pour into tall glasses and serve with a large straw.

Cucumber and yoghurt

Ingredients
3 or 4   Chopped mint leaves
½   Peeled cucumber sliced
5 fl oz (150 ml)   Carton of plain yoghurt
3 fl oz (75 ml)   Milk
Salt to taste

Method

Blend well, season to taste. Serve in tall glasses with a large straw.

Spinach and yoghurt

Ingredients
3 tablespoons   Drained cooked spinach leaf or purée
5 fl oz (150 ml)   Milk
5 fl oz (150 ml)   Carton plain yoghurt
Nutmeg to taste
Salt to taste

Method

Blend well and taste. Season again if necessary. Serve in tall glasses with a large straw.

Orange egg nog

Ingredients for 2
4   Eggs
Juice of 4 large oranges
5 fl oz (150 ml)   Carton plain yoghurt
1 dessertspoon   Sugar

Method

Beat the eggs. Add the yoghurt and the sugar and beat again. Add the orange juice and either blend or mix well. Serve in tall glasses with a straw.

Fruit cocktail

Ingredients for 3
5 fl oz (150 ml)   Apple juice
5 fl oz (150 ml)   Grape juice
5 fl oz (150 ml)   Orange juice
1 dessertspoon   Fresh or frozen strawberries
1 dessertspoon   Fresh or frozen raspberries

Method

Blend and serve in tall glasses with a straw.

✓ Watercress and tomato

Ingredients for 2
1 small bunch of watercress –
washed with roots removed
5 fl oz (150 ml)   Tomato juice
5 fl oz (150 ml)   Milk
Salt and pepper to taste

Method

Blend well and season. Pour into tall glasses and serve with a large straw.

Yoghurt, honey and egg

Ingredients for 2
2   Eggs
5 fl oz (150 ml)   Carton plain
yoghurt
5 fl oz (150 ml)   Milk
1 dessertspoon   Clear honey

Method

Blend and serve in tall glasses with a straw.

About the author

Valerie Chazan studied at Seale Hayne Agricultural College in Devon and obtained a National Diploma in Dairying. Then followed a career in veterinary and dairy bacteriology in Britain and in Israel, where she lived for 10 years. She also spent some time in the States where she picked up more recipes. On her return to England she taught home economics and broadcasted on local radio. For 8 years she bred a sizable herd of British Saanan goats, making and selling milk, cheese and yoghurt.